MY KNAPSACK IS SLUNG
The Detroit Light Guard
(1225th Corps Support Battalion)
In Iraq 2004 — 2005

By

Hrad Kuzyk

THIS IS A WARTIME BOOK

THIS EDITION WHICH IS COMPLETE
AND UNABRIDGED IS PRODUCED IN FULL
COMPLIANCE WITH THE GOVERNMENT'S
REGULATIONS FOR CONSERVING PAPER

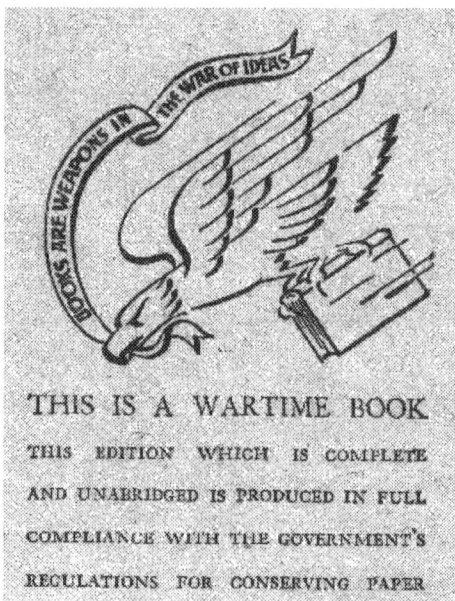

ISBN: 978-0-6151-4639-3

Photos By
SGT Ricci Moore
MSG Ronald Oakes
MSG Richard Medina
All Photos Are Used With Permission

FOR JODY GRUTZA
AND ALL OF THE OTHERS WHO HAD TO WAIT FOR US TO RETURN.
I WOULD NOT HAVE TRADED PLACES.

Table of Contents

Preface

The purpose of this book is to document the events and circumstances surrounding the deployment of the Headquarters, Headquarters Detachment, 1225th Corps Support Battalion, Michigan National Guard, in support of Operation Iraqi Freedom in 2004—2005.

This is a private endeavor by Hrad Kuzyk (formerly a captain in the 1225th CSB). It is not sponsored by any external organization, to include the 1225th CSB. CPT Kuzyk is the final arbiter in any issue stemming from this project and is solely responsible for any errors or omissions. This document will be published privately, with all funding and research provided by the author. The product of this endeavor will be sold at printing cost and will not earn a profit.

Many thanks to SGT Ricci Moore, MSG Ronald Oakes, and MSG Richard Medina for furnishing many of the pictures herein.

1225th Corps Support Battalion Crest

The shield is white, representative of Infantry, the branch of the original organization. The black arrow represents the first credited combat Indian War service of that organization. The sun and quetzal feathers, taken from the Aztec banner, represent the service of Company A at Forts Mackinac and Brady, Michigan during the Mexican War, and the palm tree is representative of service at Santiago during the Spanish-American War. The eleven mullets, or stars, are for the Civil War service. The crowned lion, taken from the Arms of Hesse, refer to the original unit's entrance into Germany during World War I.

"LET THE DRUM BEAT!"

General Hugh Brady

     The 1225th Corps Support Battalion gets its motto, "LET THE DRUM BEAT!" from the Brady Guards' namesake, General Hugh Brady. Brady was an accomplished man who is considered one of the fathers of the U.S. Army. He died on April 15, 1851, at the age of 86, following a carriage accident. As he lay dying, he was comforted by his pastor, Rev. George Duffield, who told him that his inevitable death was near. General Brady then sat straight up and offered his last words: "Mr. Duffield, **LET THE DRUM BEAT**; my knapsack is slung; I am ready to die," after which he quietly passed away.

History of the 1225th CSB
Prior to Deploying to Iraq in 2004

The unit that would serve as the first ancestor of the Headquarters and Headquarters Detachment (HHD), 1225th Corps Support Battalion (CSB), was organized during 1830 – 1831 as the Detroit City Guards and mustered into Federal service in May 1832 to fight in the Black Hawk War of 1832 against the Sauk Indians.

Reorganized in April 1836 as the Brady Guards, they were again mustered into Federal service, this time as independent companies to patrol the Canadian border during the Patriots' War of 1838 – 1839.

An element of the Brady Guards was detached and mustered into Federal service a third time in December 1847 as the First Michigan Volunteers to fight in the Mexican-American War. In this capacity, the First Michigan Volunteers fought in the battles of Cherubusco, Cerro Gordo, National Bridge, Contreras, Chapultepec, Paso Ovegos, and the City of Mexico. They were mustered out of service on July 29th, 1848.

In 1850, the Brady Guards merged with another Michigan unit, the Grayson Guards, and took their name. This organization was reorganized and redesignated as the Detroit Light Guard on November 16th, 1855.

On April 17th, 1861, five days after the Confederates initiated the Civil War by firing at Fort Sumter, the members of the Detroit Light Guard met and unanimously decided to support the Union in the upcoming fight. They were reorganized on April 25th and on May 1st, were mustered as Company A of the First Michigan Regiment. They would go on to fight in 26 actions and 11 major engagements, including the First Battle of Bull Run, Manassas, Cold Harbor, Appomattox, and the Wilderness. The First Michigan Regiment and the Detroit Light Guard were mustered out of service on July 9th, 1865, at Jeffersonville, Indiana.

After the Civil War, the Detroit Light Guard continued its military traditions and even formed a Veteran Corps of non-drilling senior soldiers who could pass valuable experience to new recruits. It was during this time that the Guard adopted the tiger's head as its mascot. This symbol was used as early as 1878 and was officially adopted on the unit crest on May 1st, 1882. (Historical evidence points to this emblem as the source of the name and logo of the Detroit Tigers baseball team.) From 1867 to 1874, the Detroit Light Guard was reorganized as independent companies of the Michigan State Troops. On December 31st, 1894, these companies were redesignated as the Michigan Guard.

On May 8th, 1898, most of the companies of the Detroit Light Guard were mustered into service and sent to fight in the Spanish-American War in Cuba, where some took part in the battles of Aguadores and Santiago.

In 1916, the Detroit Light Guard was sent to protect the U.S.-Mexican border from attacks by Pancho Villa.

In August of 1917, the Light Guard was reorganized into the 125th Infantry as a part of the Thirty-Second Division. The 125th arrived in France in January 1918 and saw action on the front in May. The newly-organized Thirty-Second Division fought in the battle of Chateau-Thierry and in the offensives of the Aisne-Marne, Soissons, Oise-Aisne, and Meuse-Argonne, where it distinguished itself. The Thirty-Second Division was decorated twice by the French government for three days' non-stop fighting, without rest, and with almost no food. In May 1919, the Light Guard was released from active duty at Camp Custer, Michigan.

The Detroit Light Guard was reorganized as the First Battalion of the First Infantry of the Michigan National Guard in 1920, and a year later was redesignated as the First Battalion of the 125th Infantry.

In October 1940, the 1/125th Infantry was reactivated into Federal service. It operated as a training unit during World War II and was also activated to quell civil disturbances throughout the 1930s, 40s, 50s, 60s, and 70s.

The 1/125th was redesignated the 425th Infantry Regiment, Michigan National Guard, in 1951, then as the 225th Infantry, Michigan National Guard, in 1960.

It was again redesignated as the 225th Quartermaster Battalion, Michigan National Guard, in 1993. This was the first time that the inheritors of the Brady Guard legacy were not infantry; they became logisticians. This unit was redesignated as the 1225th Corps Support Battalion, Michigan National Guard, in 1997, to fulfill its mission as a command element supporting supply and commodity management.

History Of The 1225th CSB
In Iraq (2004-2005)

The Headquarters, Headquarters Detachment, 1225th Corps Support Battalion was notified it was going to be deployed in April 2004. On October 8th, 2004, HHD 1225th CSB was activated and moved to Ft. McCoy, Wisconsin, for initial training and preparation for deployment. On November 27th, the advanced party arrived in Kuwait, followed by the rest of the unit on December 3rd. Within a few weeks, HHD 1225th CSB completed the requisite training in Kuwait and on or about December 19th, 2004, the entire unit had arrived at FOB Endurance (Al Qayarrah) in Iraq. Soon after, the 1225th CSB assumed authority and responsibility from the 232nd Corps Support Battalion.

During the 1225th CSB's tenure in Iraq, its basecamp would be renamed from Forward Operating Base (FOB) Endurance to Logistical Support Area (LSA) Q-West to Q-West Base Complex.

1225th CSB was originally split into three separate cells. The command cell was located at Q-West Base Complex, while one Forward Logistical Element was located at FOB Speicher (Tikrit) and another was located at LSA Diamondback (Mosul). Within a few months, both cells and all of the subordinate companies were consolidated at Q-West Base Complex.

The 1225th CSB's logistical support mission consisted of several major facets:

Transportation (Bulk Fuel for most of Northern Iraq)
Transportation (Line Haul for most of Northern Iraq)
Transportation (Gun Truck escort of TCNs)
Bulk Fuel Storage (For most of Northern Iraq)
Ammunition Storage Point (For most of Northern Iraq)
Maintenance Support
Warehouse and Hub (For most of Northern Iraq)

In addition, the 1225th CSB provided local security forces by manning security towers, running the primary Entry Control Point (ECP), and running the on-post Third Country National (TCN) holding facility, also known as "Area 51."

1225th CSB regularly convoyed to the following locations:

Q-West Base Complex (Al Qayarrah)
FOB Speicher (Tikrit)
LSA Diamondback (Mosul)
FOB Marez (Mosul)
FOB Sykes (outside Tal-Afar)
FOB Warrior (Kirkuk)
LSA Anaconda (Balad)
Fort SUSE (a detainee facility near the Iranian border)
COP Rawa (combat out-post, middle of nowhere)
Camp Zaytun (Irbil)
Civilian facilities in Dohuk

In early November 2005, HHD 1225th CSB transferred all authority to the HHD, 71st Corps Support Battalion. After returning to the United States and outprocessing through Ft. McCoy, Wisconsin, the unit was released on November 17th, 2005. They returned to their traditional home at the Detroit Light Guard Armory at 4400 East 8 Mile Road in Detroit, Michigan.

For its exceptional performance during combat operations supporting Operation Iraqi Freedom, HHD, 1225th CSB was awarded the Meritorious Unit Commendation on January 19th, 2006.

List of Units that Served with HHD, 1225th CSB

Mission	OIF 2 & OIF 2.5	OIF 3	OIF 3.5	OIF 05-07
Headquarters	HHD, 232nd CSB	HHD, 1225th CSB		HHC, 71st CSB
Bulk Fuel Storage	528th Navy POL Forward Bravo	59th Quartermaster Company		
Ammunition Supply Point		163rd Ordnance Company, Detachment F		
Transportation (Line Haul)		542nd Transportation Company		
Transportation (Line Haul)	915th Transportation Company		109th Transportation Company	
Transportation (Bulk Fuel)	454th Transportation Company	40th Transportation Company		454th Transportation Company
Transportation (Bulk Fuel)	283rd Transportation Company	360th Transportation Company		
Transportation (Bulk Fuel)	125th Transportation Company		725th Transportation Company	
Gun Truck Escort of TCNs	736th Transportation Company (Slice)			
Direct Support Maintenance	323rd Maintenance Company	818th Maintenance Company		
Warehouse and Supply Hub				305th Quartermaster Company
Convoy Medic Support		313th Medical Company (Slice)		

List of Personnel Who Served in
HHD, 1225th Corps Support Battalion in Iraq

LTC Henry C. Cason
MAJ Philip N. Estes
CPT Jeffrey Barrett
CPT Allyn A. Johnson
CPT Tiffianey J. Johnston
CPT Hrad A. Kuzyk
CPT Gregory J. Mason
CPT Matthew Neureur
CPT Kevin L. Ramey
CPT Antoine Rhodes
CPT Erick R. Schramm
CPT David M. Waskevich
Chaplain (CPT) Philip C. Willis
1LT Edith E. Feaster
1LT Jennifer Hughes
1LT Scott Scheesley
CSM Alan B. O'Leary
MSG Charles Battle
MSG Carlos Black
MSG John A. Brandau
MSG Beth Jaynes
MSG Kyle K. Krysiak
MSG Moses L. Manuel
MSG Richard Medina
MSG Ronald G. Oakes
MSG Chad E. Otte
MSG William Richardson
MSG John M. Smalenberg
MSG James R. Taylor
SFC Chantelle Baney
SFC Kevin E. Donnellon
SFC Roy Hellestro
SFC Scott Higbee
SFC Timothy J. Hoffman
SFC Anthony L. Moore
SFC Ronald E. Presnell
SFC Robert W. Price
SFC Priscilla A. Swan
SFC Noo Vang

SFC William Velez
SFC James K. Whittum
SSG Eric Blue
SSG David K. Davila
SSG Juvy B. Guico
SSG George Hathaway
SSG Venice Y. Hawkins
SSG Veronica Hill
SSG Bernard Lithkowsky
SSG Eddie Ortiz
SSG Marcus Searles
SGT Willard C. Adolph
SGT Christa M. Brown
SGT Corey L. Busby
SGT Laquinthia Carroll
SGT Anthony G. Chavalia
SGT Diedra Cook
SGT Lalillian Y. Haynes
SGT Anthony G. Houston
SGT Megan McDougal
SGT Matthew McGonigal
SGT Ricci E. Moore
SGT Renee M. Muns
SGT Ansgar Olsen
SGT Lydell O. Tinnon
SGT Scott L. Wilkens
SGT Kevin A Whitfield
SPC Jennifer J. Allen
SPC Deborah M. Anderson
SPC Ajeenah I. Ansari
SPC Dazarine L. Bell
SPC Maria Byrd
SPC Brian E. Holt
SPC Brittanni D. Ott
SPC Chanda T. Rogers
SPC David D. Rogers
SPC Raymond B. Sanders
SPC Phillip L. Sangster
SPC Cierra R. Sly
SPC Lashandia C. Willis
SPC Guy T. Wilson
MAJ Steven E. Stapleton
MAJ Bryan S. Franklin

Fallen Soldiers of the
1225th Corps Support Battalion

SSG Brian Morris (360th TC)
SGT Julio Negron (360th TC)
SPC Gavin Colburn (542nd TC)
SPC Lizbeth Robles (360th TC)
PFC Elden Arcand (360th TC)

Pictures of
HHD, 1225th CSB
In Iraq

Headquarters Headquarters Detachment, 1225th Corps Support Battalion in Iraq in 2005

HHD, 1225th CSB Supporting The Home Team

HHD, 1225th CSB Showing Thanks for Free Chrysler T-Shirts

HHD Soldiers at Ft. McCoy Signing for Equipment that is the Wrong Size

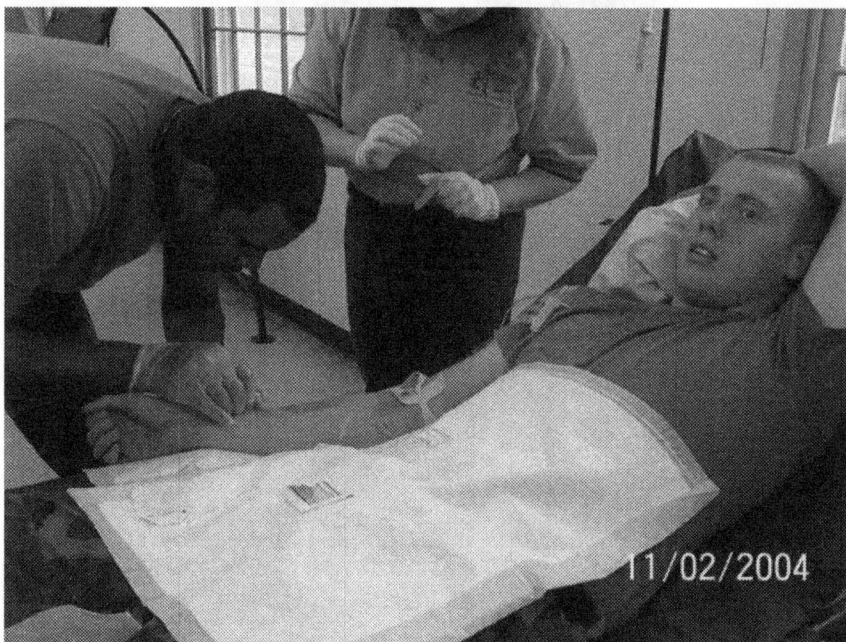
SPC Rogers Practices Inserting an IV into the Arm of a Training Dummy
SPC Holt at Ft. McCoy, Wisconsin

11/03/2004

SPC Sangster Rehearsing a One-Man Carry on a Reluctant SGT Moore

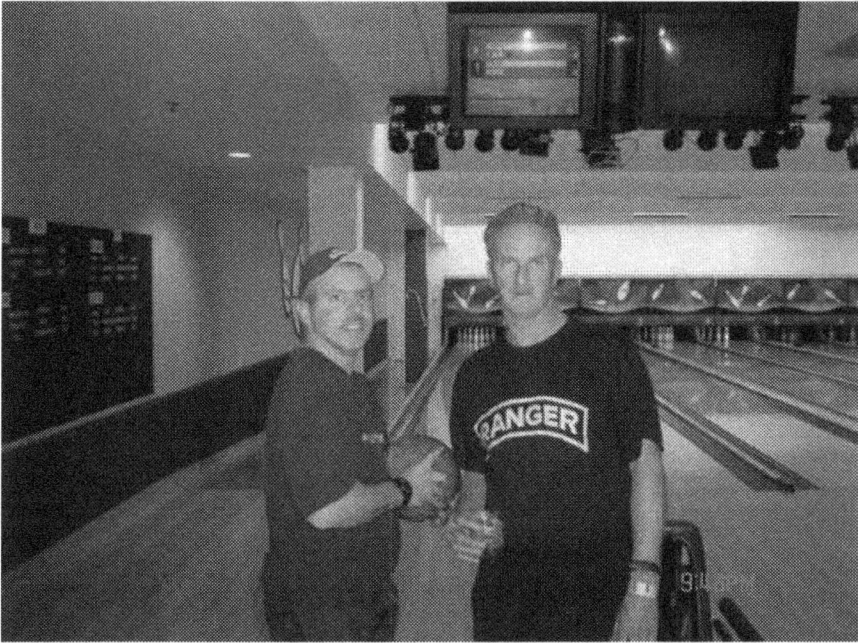

SFC Donnellon and SFC Hoffman Bowling and Drinking at McCoy's

SSG Davila at Ft. McCoy Training to Fight in the Hot Desert

HHD Conducting Convoy Lanes Training in Kuwait

SPC Sangster Preparing for ~~Hollywood~~ Iraq

HHD Soldiers on a C-130 Flying from Kuwait into Iraq

HHD 1225th CSB Sign at Q-West Base Complex

SSG Guico and MSG Oakes Preparing to Go on a Convoy

HHD Formation at Q-West Base Complex

SFC Price and SFC Hoffman Building the MWR Room

CSM O'Leary, LTC Cason, Iraqi General Ali, and Another Iraqi Officer

CPT Ramey, SFC Swan, and SFC Hoffman

MSG Oakes with Iraqi Army Guards

SGT Houston, SPC Rogers, SSG Hathaway, SPC Holt, and SPC Wilson
Kneeling: SPC Willis

MSG Brandau, SFC Hoffman, and SFC Whittum on the BN HQ Roof

HHD Gun Truck HQ-9 (Half Factory Armor, Half Homemade Armor)

In Front of the BN HQ Building During the Rainy Season

HHD Motor Pool Parking Area with Unidentified Cone (WMD?)

Containerized Housing Units (CHUs) Outside of the HQ Building

CHUs Outside of the HQ Building

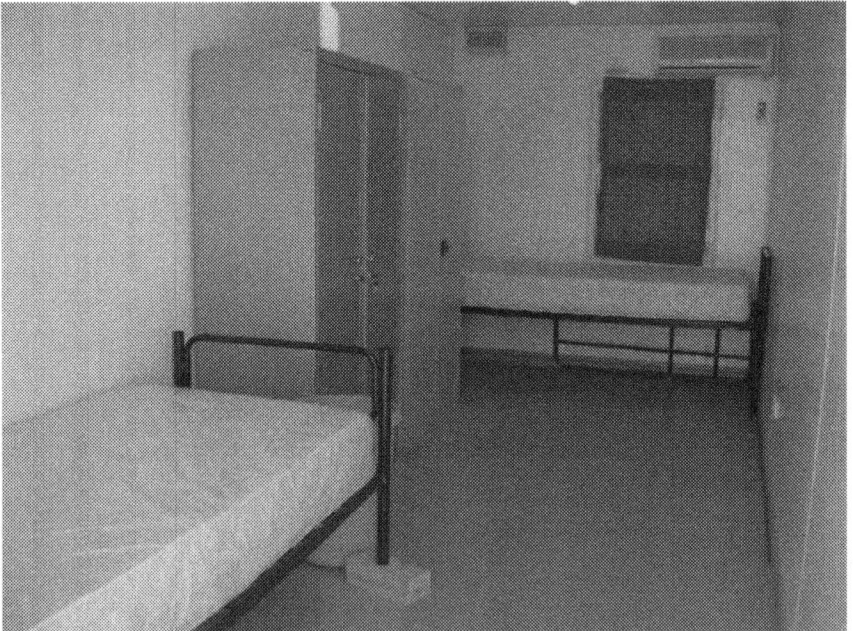
Inside of a Typical 2-Person CHU

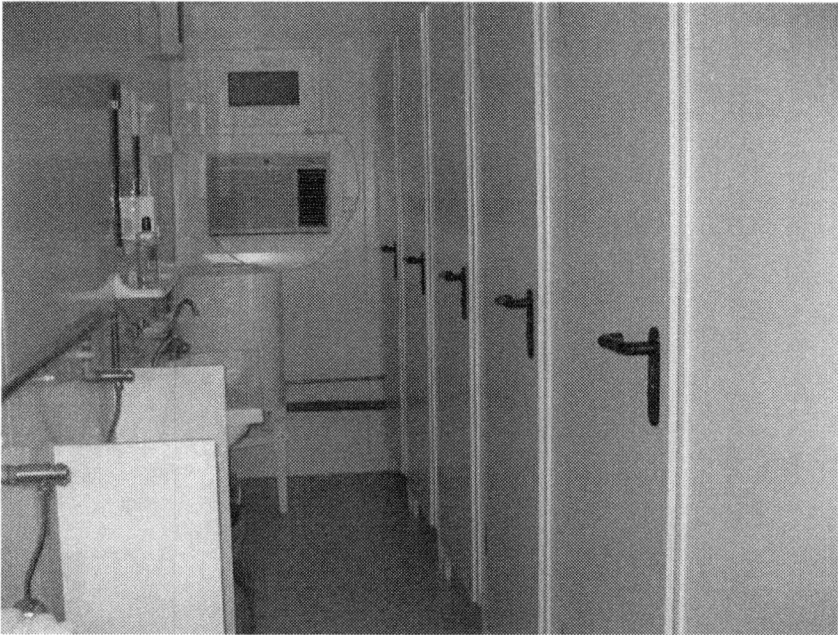
Inside of a CHU Adapted as a Toilet Unit

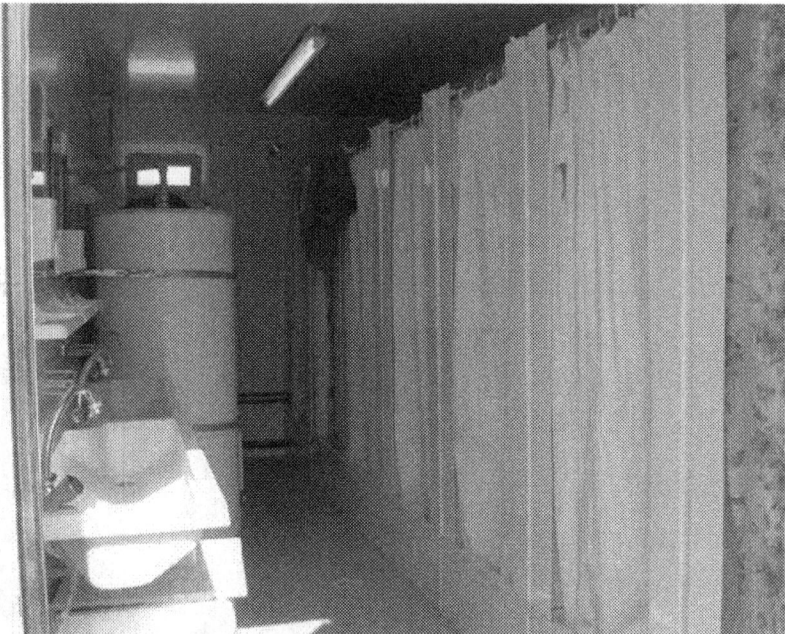
Inside of a CHU Adapted as a Shower Unit

Blown-Up "Palace" at Q-West Base Complex

Blackhawk Helicopter and Soldiers Going On Leave

HHD Soldiers at the Q-West Base Complex Dining Facility

~~SGT Tinnon Captures An Insurgent~~
SGT Tinnon and SFC Swan Showing the Love

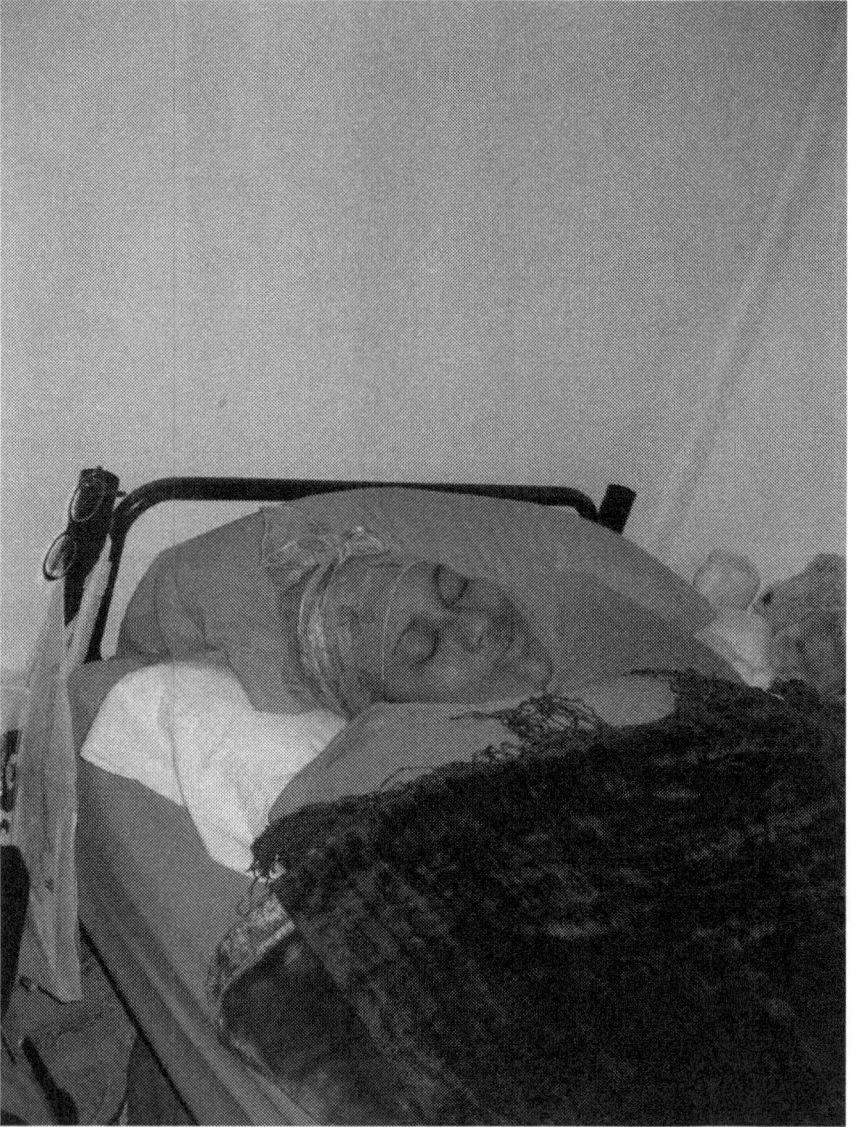

SPC Ansari Demonstrating Tactical Sleeping Gear

LTC Cason Promoting SFC Oakes to MSG Oakes

LTC Cason Promoting SGT Guico to SSG Guico

SPC Tinnon, SPC Sly, and CPT Kuzyk

CPT Kuzyk and CPT Ramey Hard at Work Planning
Future Logistical Contingency Operations at Q-West in Iraq

SPC Whitfield, SFC Moore, SPC Carroll, CPT Hughes, SGT Tinnon,
and CPT Rhodes

SPC Holt Pondering the Meaning of Life
on the C-130 Flight Leaving from Iraq to Kuwait

HHD Soldiers in Kuwait Loading Personal Gear for the Flight Home

Some Faces of
HHD, 1225th CSB Soldiers
in Iraq

SPC Deborah Anderson

SPC Ajeenah Ansari

SPC Dazarine Bell

MSG John Brandau

SGT Christa Brown

SGT Corey Busby

LTC Henry Cason

SGT Anthony Chavalia

SSG David Davila

SFC Kevin Donnellon

MAJ Philip Estes

1LT Edith Feaster

SSG Juvy Guico

SSG George Hathaway

SSG Venice Hawkins

SGT Lalillian Haynes

SFC Timothy Hoffman

SPC Brian Holt

SGT Anthony Houston

CPT Allyn Johnson

CPT Tiffianey Johnston

MSG Kyle Krysiak

CPT Hrad Kuzyk

SFC Anthony Moore

MSG Richard Medina

SGT Renee Muns

MSG Ronald Oakes

CSM Alan O'Leary

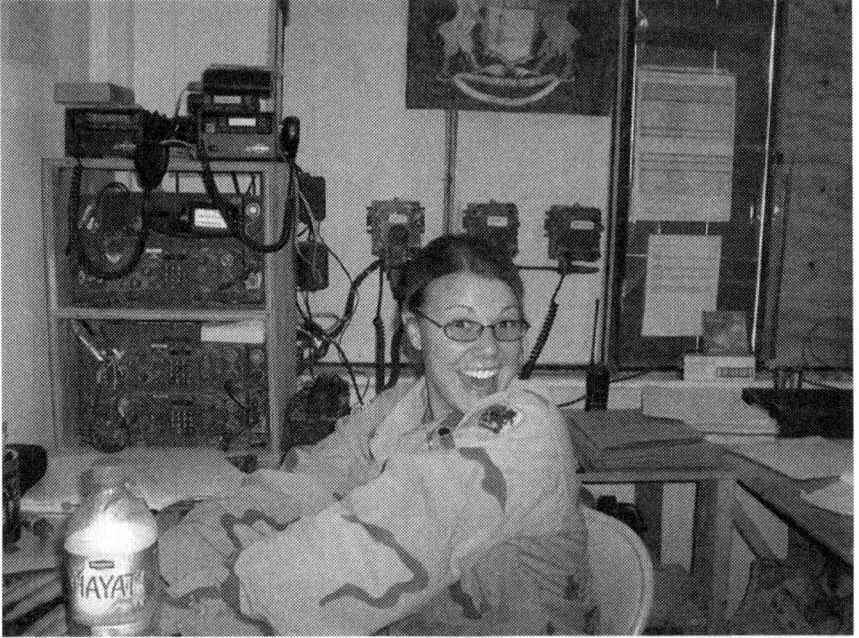

SGT Brittanni Ott

SFC Ronald Presnell

SFC Robert Price

CPT Kevin Ramey

MSG William Richardson

SPC Chanda Rogers

SPC David Rogers

SPC Raymond Sanders

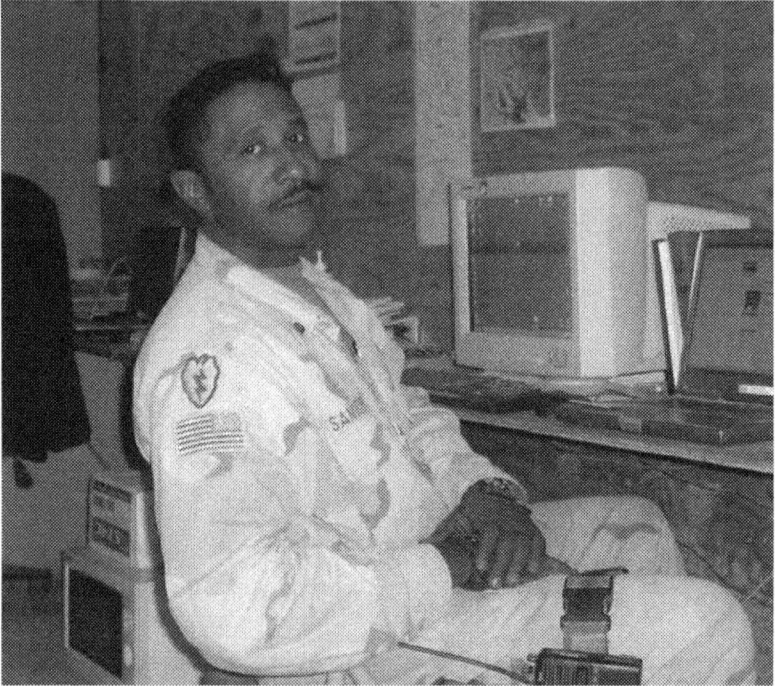

SPC Phillip Sangster

CPT Erick Schramm

SPC Cierra Sly

MSG John Smalenberg

SFC Priscilla Swan

MSG James Taylor

SGT Lydell Tinnon

CPT David Waskevich

SGT Kevin Whitfield

SFC James Whittum

SGT Scott Wilkens

SPC Lashandia Willis

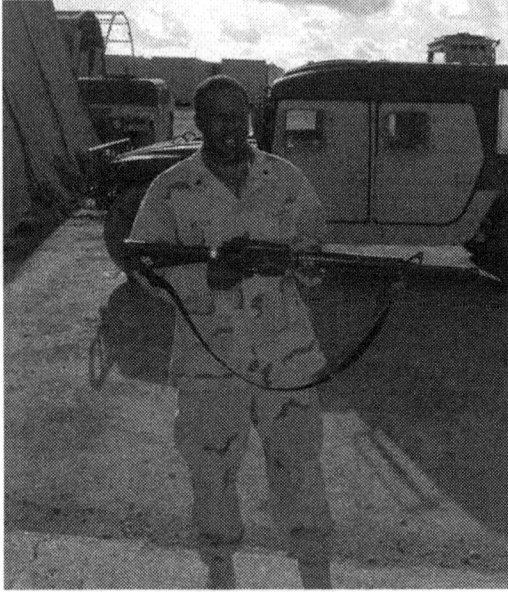

SPC Guy Wilson

www.ingramcontent.com/pod-product-compliance
Lightning Source LLC
Chambersburg PA
CBHW020519030426
42337CB00011B/466